2/22/23

~~Allen~~

So glad to
share some
thoughts and
words with you

Henry

A Soul Laid Bare

Writings
from a Questioning Mind

NANCY E. WOLCOTT

*"Words [spoken] dazzle and deceive
because they are mimed by the face.
But black words on a white page
are the soul laid bare."*

(Guy de Maupassant)

Kindle Direct Publishing ISBN: 9798835771547

*"Write only if you cannot live without writing.
Write only what you alone can write."*

(Elie Wiesel)

*"Let yourself go.
Pull out from the depths those thoughts
that you do not understand,
and spread them out in the sunlight,
and know the meaning of them."*

(E.M. Forster)

"Writing is a socially acceptable form of schizophrenia."

(E.L. Doctorow)

Contents

Introduction

MY PERSONALIZED TWIST ON DESCARTES' proposition "I think, therefore I am" is: "I think, therefore I write." I could also say: I'm impassioned, therefore I write; I have doubts, therefore I write; I'm confused, therefore I write. Whatever the provocation, I have always written—initially to understand my thoughts and eventually to express them.

Embedding black words on white pages, with ink or keyboard, is the only way for me to free my mind enough to contemplate what was weighing on it. And if that's true for me, clearly it must be the impetus for other writers. So next I read whatever I can get my hands on that others have written about similar doubts or passions or questions. Which takes me back to my writing, editing endlessly.

Sometimes there's an Ah-Ha moment in the cycle, sometimes not, but I'm convinced I evolve a little with each writing. The process becomes my continuing education, and hopefully part of a gradual transformation into whoever it is I was destined to be.

Now in my 75th year of life, I've started thinking about what I should do with all these writings, at the same time that I'm wondering how I would like people to remember me when I'm gone. And so, I've selected and categorized some favorites—poetry and prose, analogy and satire, lessons learned, and snippets from a never-ending journey of faith—to share primarily with family and friends; but, because I'm self-publishing it through Amazon KDP, also with people who will only know me through these words.

I hope those who read this will come away with some thoughts worth pondering and maybe even encouragement to put their own thoughts into written words. If nothing else, you will have a better picture of a human being who struggles and perseveres; a melancholic individual with a sense of humor who is nothing if not honest; and a soul who, despite doubts and questions of faith, gratefully experiences the embrace of her Creator.

Note that when I say I "edit endlessly," that includes editing the writings in this book beyond the date indicated with each writing. For example, I may have even added an evil Putin into writings written before his invasion of the Ukraine.

I majored in English in college, so here's my take: *English majors never die; they save themselves in words.*

And here's a good summary of who I think I am:

> *"There was a gray-haired lady,*
> *a few years south of eighty,*
> *with an age-spot in the middle of her forehead.*
> *And when she was kind, she was very, very kind;*
> *but when she was judgmental, she was horrid!"*

(nw)

WRITING

"The best [writing] comes from someplace deep inside.
You don't write because you want to,
but because you have to."

(Judy Blume)

Motivation

5/15/14, nw

When inspired by perspective,
provoked by a passion,
or lured by melancholic genes,
I write.

I write, motivated not by arbitrary thoughts,
but by kindled emotions
assuaged only through
the precise selection of words.

Unless I can capture
and engrave
the vision created by these thoughts,
I remain unsettled.

Not until each decisive word
fits comfortably next to another,
refined through copious edits
and preserved in ink,
is my urgency defined and vented.

Only then does the excitement,
the vexation, the despondency recede—
albeit briefly—
along with a compelling need
to give voice to my demons and passions.

A Gift of Solitude

1/10/97, nw

Some days my name is Silence.
Not aloofness. Not indifference.
I am not angry or offended,
just gratefully alone.

I cast aside the risks
of social interaction,
to hide myself away—
wrapped in longed-for solitude.

And then I use the gifts replete within me
to listen, ponder, write, and seek.
To let my thoughts become inspired
and emerge in written form.

A soul laid bare.
A gift from the Divine! A beam of light
piercing the barrier of finitude.
Perhaps a glimmer of eternity.

Capturing the Moment

6/14/14, nw

Escape.
Projects, problems, dirty laundry,
someone else's bitterness
… left behind.

An unencumbered weekend on the southern coast of Maine;
rhododendrons in full bloom,
the scent of honeysuckle,
a good book, my journal,
and the man I love
… but more importantly, the man who loves me.

Real old-fashioned wicker chairs on the veranda
of a charming old Victorian B & B,
and the need to capture the moment in written words
inspired by sea air and wild roses.

*(Written on Mark's and my first anniversary weekend get-away
to the Inn at Tanglewood Hall in York, Maine.)*

In Defense of Punctuation

5/31/12, nw

To those of us obsessed with the message:
Punctuation is paramount!

It is the cadence of our thoughts
once translated into words—
spoken, written, and read.

Punctuation is the medium
through which we express
emotion, tone, inference.
Hesitation…
Confusion?
Certainty.

It is a box of tools
with which we fine-tune our message.
Tools that enable us to
illuminate, elaborate, define,
ask, sing,
pause…
avoid ambiguity.

The multi-tasking comma,
the definitive colon.
The thoughtful semicolon;
the overused en dash.
The underused em dash—
Rambling ellipses . . .
Clarifying parentheses

Exclamation points!
Question marks?
The (technically not punctuation
but nevertheless)
breath-taking
line break!

The final period.

Punctuation marks are symbols
giving voice to the words
that capture our thoughts.

"I am struck by how sharing our weakness and difficulties is more nourishing to others than sharing our qualities and successes."

(Jean Vanier)

"The beginning of wisdom is to call things by their right names."

(Chinese Proverb)

CHALLENGE

"*When you come out of the storm, you won't be the same person who walked in. That's what this storm's all about.*"

(Haruki Murakami, *Kafka on the Shore*)

"*We cannot heal what we do not first acknowledge.*"

(Richard Rohr)

Soft and Hard

3/29/02, nw

MY MOTHER HAD TWO FACES. The one I loved and longed for was soft and beautiful, gentle and kind. The one I feared was troubled; defined by frustration and uncertainty. I never knew which side of my mother I would see when I came home from school each day. I hoped, of course, for the mother who would ask and actually care about my day; who would smile a lot and tell me funny memories of me or her. The mother who would encourage me and help me and try to understand me.

But I would know—the minute she turned her face in my direction. She didn't have to say a word. The dreaded side of my mother would manifest itself in the downward turn of her mouth, the hardened stare from her eyes, the clench of her jaw, her chiseled, unbending stature. And I would take on the responsibility of her demeanor. I would convince myself that this hardened personality must somehow be my fault. Maybe that was the only way I could accept that side of my mother. . . by taking the blame away from her.

My father and two older brothers seemed to pretend my mother wasn't "home" when she was like that. They would carefully avoid her and she would avoid all of us, as an eerie silence filled our home. I would hide in my room for as long as possible with my mother's mood weighing me down—seeping into my very being—until finally I would walk into her space and let her unburden.

But it wasn't always like that. There were happy, healthy family days, when my mother's other face would shine, her dark mood mysteriously and gratefully gone, her smile and gentle spirit penetrating our family and home. She would laugh at my father's corny jokes and flirts, and my brothers and I could stop tiptoeing around. I'm sure there were triggers that would take her to her dark place, but my father, brothers and I lived for her happy days, her happy face.

"Depression" was a hidden word in the 1950s and 60s, and certainly before. Actually, I'm not sure I ever understood it until the 1970s—when I began to realize it applied to me as well. The term "bi-polar" hadn't been invented yet. How did my mother define or even begin to comprehend her dark moods in an era when counseling was shameful and anti-depressants were unheard of?

In her later years, I was less and less aware of her moods, and before her death from cancer at the age of 63, her dark days seemed to be a thing of the past. The framed photos of my mother throughout my home show a beautiful person of purpose and value; no darkness evident. Cracking a smile at age three; looking serious and sophisticated in her high school graduation photo; suppressing an inner beam in her engagement portrait; and barely concealing her pride at the age of 58 as she earned her bachelor's degree.

A Beautiful Mask

7/9/15, nw

I WAS TRYING TO ACT COOL and all-together as I chatted with my counselor, Carol, yesterday during my mid-week appointment.

"You know me so well," I said with a chuckle, after she responded to one of my self-flagellating jokes.

"I do," she replied. "You take off your beautiful mask when you come to my office and let me get to know the real you."

A "beautiful mask." (Long pause while that sinks in to the brain behind the mask.) That's what I am. That's what I do. I wear a mask that I have honed to grammatical, social, and physical-correctness over almost seven decades of life.

A "beautiful mask" is a perfect summation of everything I try to be—except the real me. For most of my life I have been a shiny façade that made my parents proud and continues to fool people into thinking I'm all-together, resilient, content . . . and "so perfect" (as some have disparagingly described me to others).

But I am none of those things. For too long I have felt so *imperfect*, so fake, with the fear that no one would like the real me, should she emerge someday.

The true irony is that this well-honed mask goads me into judging people who actually are quite resilient and content in their identity; people who don't need to put on masks.

Example: Amy, a neighbor who lives across the street, comes out of her house with a beer in her hand, wearing tight spandex clothing that reveals a slightly bulging body, and sits on her porch, feet propped up on a table. With a raucous laugh, she jokingly tells her adult son to "Get [his] shit together!"

Everything Nancy the Mask would NEVER do.

But I hate my Mask.

If only I had the guts to be an unabashed Amy.

How many times in my life have I wished I was from a different family structure, culture or class or background, or planet, or that I was homely or handicapped or physically disfigured—so that the inner me had nothing to hide behind? So that I could get to know and like (instead of judging) real people who don't need masks? People with different standards and features and strengths and flaws and habits and hopes and goals. So that I could get to know—and be content with—myself?

As my hair turns gray and age spots begin to decorate my body, I'm comforted with the realization that my mask is pealing off, however gradually. I'm starting to know, admit to, and even laugh at the not-so-perfect me—and appreciate the differences in others.

"Write what disturbs you, what you fear, what you have not been willing to speak about. Be willing to be split open."

(Natalie Goldberg)

Confronting Our Walls
4/27/17, nw

FROM THE MINUTE WE'RE BORN, from the first breath we take, we face challenges. Life is a challenge. But were it not for obstacles in our lives in need of being addressed, we would be stunted individuals, far from our potential. Our bodies would grow into adult stature, but the person we were created to become would remain sadly underdeveloped.

A baby is born. Like it or not, going back to the warmth and security of the womb is no longer an option. She's never known hunger, but now she does; and confront it, she must. There's not much else she can do at that early stage of life but cry—an instinctual, but still confrontive action. And in each succeeding stage of growth she'll confront her hunger and other issues more creatively, depending on what produces the best results.

Ideally, children and adolescents face and learn to address challenges as a natural and necessary part of the growth process. But the older we get, the more we rebel at that which makes us unhappy or uncomfortable, and the more excuses we're likely to make.

A scowl on my face or your face represents an emotion, along the lines of frustration or anger or depression or embarrassment or guilt or worry.

On the other side of this emotion—way over there—I can see the sun shining and people going on with their lives just as I desperately want to go on with my life—but I'm stuck. I can't go forward because there is a wall, a challenge in my way and I don't know how to take it down!

Someone comes up to me and says, "What's happenin'?" I turn to them, manage to fake a smile, and say, "Oh, Hi! I'm fine; how are you?" The person gives a thumbs up, walks over to where the sun is shining (no barrier in their path!), and goes on with their life, while I'm stuck here in my rut.

One day, another friend stops by and points out that I seem a little frustrated (… angry, depressed, worried, or some such emotion). "Yup. You're right," I respond. "I am struggling with something. And it's preventing me from moving on."

And I think to myself, "I've got to give a name to this wall and deal with it!"

Here is a true and relevant illustration: I realized I was becoming more and more critical of the people in my life. Maybe it was (my opinion of) their politics, their personal habits, their tendency to exaggerate (unlike me, of course). But this increasingly critical nature conflicts with my desire to be a kind and loving person. So, I identify the wall facing me as "Judgmentalism." Good place to start. I have given it a name and it has clicked into my brain that I need to confront it.

I become sensitive to my newly identified walls, more careful to prevent what they represent, and more constructively repentant.

Perhaps I've identified my wall as Jealousy. Or Condescension. Or Close-mindedness. Self-Centeredness. Disrespectfulness. Lying. Addiction. Laziness. Impatience. Overeating . . . .

The best consequence of getting into the habit of identifying and addressing our own individual walls/ issues/ shortcomings is that we eventually stop focusing on everyone else's!

"First, remove the beam from your own eye, and then you can see clearly to remove the speck out of your brother's eye." (Matthew 7:5)

Now to address my habit of starting written sentences with conjunctions . . . .

Introspection

5/28/14, nw

Today,
the very dollop of disapproval
flung at me yesterday and rebuffed,
would hit my fragile psyche like a bullet.

Why is that?
Why do I so often fall
when other days I stand?

Today,
criticism breaks me.
The hint of judgment shakes me.
I over-compensate; I over-react.
I brace myself; I cringe.
And if I sense a whiff of disappointment
my inner core curls up.
My smile fades, my head sinks,
and a voice between my ears berates me.

Where is my self-esteem on days like this?
Why was my yesterday strong,
yet my today so fragile?

"Hello," my inner voice reasons.
"If someone else's dollop of disapproval
can knock you down today,
what about your thoughtlessly flung dollops
on other days?"

Introspection.
Is it laden with a dollop of guilt . . .
or buoyed with a dollop of understanding?
Am I moving backward or forward?
Inward or outward?
Is it focus on myself
or compassion for others?

Today I am contemplative.
Tomorrow I may be other wise,
or foolish.

So wait!
Tomorrow my rebuffing shield may be in place
and I won't need to write these words,
or think these thoughts, or
worry about dollops, mine or yours.

Perception of Truth
11/24/13, nw

There is perception:
"It's a cloudy day."

And there is conjecture:
"It's supposed to be cloudy for the next few days."

There is opinion:
"Cloudy days are depressing."

And there is theory:
"People tend to be less happy on cloudy days."

There is fact:
"Absence of sunlight produces a mood suppressant."

And there is diplomacy:
"Even when obstructed by clouds, the sun is shining."

There is optimism:
"Tomorrow may be a sunny day."

And there is gratitude:
"If it weren't for cloudy days, I wouldn't appreciate sunny days."

And then . . . there is truth.
"Sunny days are worth waiting for."

Reflections

4/6/07, nw

On days when I don't like myself,
I look in the mirror and see a person who is
crabby, old, wrinkled, fat, flabby, and flawed;
mindless, clueless, fearful, bitter, and spiteful;
selfish and self-pitying.
I am, on those days,
absorbed in myself…
how I look
inside and out.
And it just
    ain't
        pretty.

On days when I like who I am
(difficult as it is to remember on days when I don't)
it's not me or what I look like that matters,
but whom I am reflecting.
On those days,
I am becoming less,
you are becoming more.
There's love instead of bitterness;
trust instead of spite;
joy instead of pity.
And I
    am absorbed
        in you.

The Two of Me

1/21/07, nw

There are two of me…

The me I like
is milestone dots upon an upward climb;
Joshua before the Promised Land.
A heart set free.
Loved, forgiven, and with purpose.

But all it takes is a trigger
for the other me to fall.

A critical word,
a hard memory,
Thoughtlessness—mine or yours—
And I am down for the count.

Questioning my worth,
I isolate myself,
desperate for a sighting
of the Promised Land.

Anger Bordering on Rage

10/3/18, nw

I AM AN EDUCATED, intelligent, retired 71-year-old woman who is feeling anger bordering on rage spilling out as I
watch our nation's current POTUS and SCOTUS debacles.

The Supreme Court nomination and televised hearings
for Brett Kavanaugh have ripped open personal wounds carefully covered over through years of denial. Wounds that contributed to a poor self-esteem for most of my life.

I immediately identified with the "Me Too" movement
when it started, and I would nod my head in silence. But I
have been silent for far too long. I want to roar! So, instead,
I'll write.

To those of you who knew me as a student at Lower More-
land High School in the early 1960s, I have returned to my
maiden name with pride. If you are Danny or Eddie, does my
name ring a bell?

Danny, did you know I had never seen a penis until you
pulled yours out of your pants on our first and only date at a
drive-in movie? What did you think I was going to do with
it? I wish I had been bold and angry and confident enough to
say, "You are a pervert and an idiot, and if you don't put your
ugly dick back in your pants I'll cut it off!" But I had no idea
what you were even suggesting, let alone what I was supposed
to do—not to mention that that's pretty far from the type of
response I learned in my upbringing. Was it some rite of pas-
sage? Was there an appropriate response for a fifteen-year-old
girl to give when some guy pulls out his penis? I remember
turning and looking out the passenger window for a long
time, wishing that image would erase itself from my mind. It
didn't. In fact, that image has seared itself in my memory for

over 50 years.

And Eddie, if you should happen to read this, you were the first boy to give me a "friendship" ring, which came with your explanation of what "going steady" meant—that you had the right to go at least to "first base" with me, and to "second base" if we hit it off. You and your big brother with whom we double-dated would make fun of my "big boobie" shape each time I would get in the car. And I would wonder what I was supposed to do or say, because I thought every girl who was going steady had to go through this; and I wanted to be accepted as a "normal" girl; a "popular" girl.

To the single-minded fraternity guys in college . . . please consider what wisdom you might offer to your grandsons and granddaughters as they enter college.

And to the psychiatrist I went to see when I was going through a significant identity crisis as a 23-year-old in the early 1970s: I don't remember your name, but I will never forget the words you used to proposition me after I told you how I struggled with the stigma of being a flight attendant. When I asked why you were not responding to what I was saying, you put your elbows on your desk and folded your hands and said, "Because I want to 'ball you'." Instead of saying "Excuse me?!," I should have said "Oh, is 'ball you' the preferred term among educated psychiatrists when they want to have intercourse with their female patients who are trying to describe their identity struggle in a 'man's world'—when all they want is acceptance and a sense of value?" I should have slapped the glasses off your face. I should have reported you to…to… to whom? To whom did women in the 1970s or the 1980s or the 1990s, or until very recently report sexual assault or harassment?? Instead I walked out of your office thinking I was nothing more than an object to be played with by horny men.

I was not a person of worth or integrity or purpose. I was, as Danny and Eddie and a lecherous psychiatrist wanted me to be, an object . . . not a person.

And to those older men in supervisory positions employed by Univac and the Armstrong Cork Company when I was still trying to get through my professional twenties, why did I allow you to make sexual accusations and jokes and come-ons at my expense? Why did I tip-toe away feeling dirty and somehow responsible for your vile implications? Why didn't I see your repulsive comments and actions as what they were? Why didn't/ couldn't I report them? Gee, I wonder why I didn't consider going to see some sort of a mental health professional??

But, "Providence" was on my side and I finally "came to the Lord" in the 1970s Jesus Movement. I was so "on fire for the Lord" that I was convinced I should go to seminary, where I met Richard, that dashing seminarian from New Zealand who helped me see the light . . . and a few other things. Yes, he confirmed that intercourse outside of marriage was biblically wrong, but the Bible doesn't say anything's wrong with certain other things, now does it? I was a "new believer", after all, and I always believed what those "more mature believers" told me. I was also extremely naive.

Just before earning my MA in Theological Studies, I met another seminarian who asked me to marry him. Praise be! A little over halfway through our 24-year-marriage, my husband felt compelled to tell me he thought I might have "the spirit of Jezebel." *That* was a new phrase in my ever-broadening Christian vocabulary, and one that required me to make a list for my husband of all the men with whom I had ever had any kind of sexual experience . . . for the sake of our "biblically-correct" marriage. So, naïve Nancy obeyed. My honest list raised his eyebrows well beyond his biblically-correct forehead, and there wasn't a whole lotta' mutual respect in our marriage from then on before we finally divorced. I eventually left the church for various reasons, but a 2008 Newsweek Magazine cover sums it up. The cover title was: "Evangelical Women Worship Sarah Palin." When I made my disagreement and frustration evident to my church, clearly I had left the fold.

Fortunately, despite *my* issues, testosterone issues, and society's issues, I also remember other men in my life with great respect. I think of Johnny and Tim and Joey and Steve and other boys in my high school who treated me with kindness and equality. I think of my brothers, Chip and Bill, who watched out for their little sister. I think of my dad, who loved and respected me with the purest and most meaningful fatherly love, and made me feel of value. I think of Derek in college who, when I asked him why he loved me, quoted Sherwood Anderson, saying "You must not try to make love definite; it is the divine accident of life." And I think especially of my husband, Mark, who loves me in so many noble, kind, and significant ways—and has restored my sense of worth.

Times have changed. Little by little, inch by painful inch, women have gained ground and respect and recognition— and a very important voice. We need to let our voices be heard for all the right reasons. In fact, I believe we should roar, if we need to; if it will bring with it constructive, redemptive, and healing change for our daughters and sons, and grandchildren, and our world. And, if it will renew our own personal sense of value and worth.

"I believe as each woman tells her story for the first time, she breaks the silence, and by doing so breaks her isolation, begins to melt her shame and guilt . . . lifting her pain."

(Eve Ensler)

The Art of Healing

8/2/15, nw

After the fall,
the mistake,
the departure, the disloyalty,
the criticism, the estrangement,
the wound—whatever it might be,

comes the pain, the anger,
the fear, the denial,
the consequences.

And then the scab,
the crusting over.
Regret . . . and sadness.
The ugly time.
Nothing on the surface looks or feels good

until healing begins;
the pain recedes,
the scar becomes a memory of a weaker time,
a badge of forgiveness
allowing the renewal of strength
and love,
and growth.

A Family Story

2/23/09, nw

MANY YEARS AGO, in a village in Matabeleland, a man named Puti lived with his wife and two children.

Puti was not the village chief, but he felt he was as wise as the village chief, and so, in his mind, he saw himself as important, intelligent, and . . . big. (Sometimes Puti would think about his childhood and how his father had made him feel unimportant. But that would be another story.)

Puti's wife had different ways of looking at life. Sometimes others in the village would say to her: "Your thoughts are interesting. Thank you for speaking them." But this would make Puti unhappy and he would sulk. His wife would sense his displeasure. (She was a person who had always struggled to find worth in herself. But, that too, would be another story to tell another time.)

One day, when the family was eating their mid-day meal, the mother suggested they play a game after eating. Puti folded his arms and said: "No. We will not do that."

When his wife asked him why, he became angry that she would question his decision. So he turned to her and said sternly: "Because I disagree!"

Puti's wife knew that, in her culture, the husband was the head of the family and that she should not question him; she must submit to his wishes. Feeling sadness and a sense of low worth, she walked away and went into her hut. She lay down on her mat and covered herself for warmth.

When Puti saw this, he felt . . . stronger . . . and . . . bigger. And, so, the next time his wife made a suggestion, he did the very same thing. He crossed his arms and glared at his wife and said: "No. I disagree."

The children watched as this pattern grew. They would see their father cross his arms and straighten his shoulders, and they would see the look of disdain in his eyes as he spoke to their mother. When he would end a conversation with his her by saying "I disagree," the children would notice that their father held his head higher and a very small smile was on his lips.

On another day, when the family was again having their noon meal together, the mother said to her son, "Finish what is in your bowl so it will not be wasted."

Usually the little boy was respectful and obedient, but this time the words "I disagree!" came angrily out of his mouth. This was such an unusual response for a child to make to a parent in Matabeleland, that everyone in the family stopped eating and looked at the boy—and then at the mother. The mother said, "That is disrespectful. You must not answer your mother in that way."

The little boy folded his arms and glared at her, refusing to eat or respond. After a few minutes, the mother turned to her husband and said, "Please, husband, speak to your son." Puti looked from his wife to the boy, but said nothing. Instead he stood up and walked away.

The boy and girl turned their eyes to their mother. She arose and walked to her hut. And there was silence.

Now alone together, the sister noticed a slight smile on her brother's face, as he straightened his shoulders and lifted up his chin.

I have written this story in the simplest of words and placed it in an uncomplicated culture to help me try to understand what I walked away from in the fall of 2003.

I didn't walk away from a tribal patriarchal family or village in

Matabeleland (a region in modern-day Zimbabwe), but from a contemporary, evangelical Christian marrirage and church structure in New Hampshire. The wife from the village in Matabeleland could never have left.

I didn't really walk away as much as I crept away, shadowed by the confusing traditions that defined me until then. Once separated from my husband, I learned to survive, one day at a time, in a new place with new friends and an opening mind. Eventually I left the church where I had been expected to be submissive and not question doctrine, and I began a journey of faith that has emboldened me to ask questions and seek answers in new ways, and to understand who I was created to be.

"Most people want to forget.
Don't forget things that were painful or embarrassing or silly.
Turn them into a story that tells the truth."

(Paula Danziger)

Better Thoughts

1/30/18, nw

MANY OF MY RANDOM WRITINGS descend into a folder on my hard drive called "Melancholic Thoughts." But I'm thinking I should start tracking my "Better Thoughts." As in: "OK, so this may not be a good day, but what one positive thing I can focus on?" So here goes.

Day One:
I'm pretty sure I've screwed up as a mother. My depressive episodes and related issues have contributed significantly to that. *But, my husband Mark loves me. He loves me despite my moods; despite my low self-esteem; despite my you-deserve-better-than-me arguments. He wants to go through all this with me. Wow. Someone thinks I have worth!*

Day Two:
The persistent thought that I may never be reconciled to my daughter Laura overwhelms me. *Yet, time still exists for healing to take place. If it doesn't happen in my lifetime, this hard lesson has definitely humbled me—and that's a good thing, right?*

Day Three:
There are times, in my wide range of moods swings, when I long for a diagnosis of stage 4 terminal cancer or an inoperable brain aneurism. I realize that such a diagnosis, especially at my whim, is unlikely—due to my stubborn conviction that *according to God I have value, and apparently God is not quite finished with me yet. In which case, I'm fortunate to have good health as I enter another decade of life.*

Letter to Laura

8/7/17, nw

Tomorrow you'll begin another year of life.

May it be peaceful, yet exciting;
eye opening, astounding, enlightening,
inspirational, profound, curious;
educational, insightful, productive, and happy.
Filled with love and the opportunity to love;
successful, yet challenging.
May you learn from mistakes.
May you grow from disappointments.
May you find new avenues of hope and courage
and creativity and kindness and giving.

I went up into the attic today to look for an old ink swatch.
I didn't find it, but I sat for a long while with boxes labeled
"Laura Childhood", "Laura High School" and "Laura Save".

It gave me hope and reason to trust
that sorrow and forgiveness and healing
might be manifested in beautiful new ways
for both of us
in this new year of your life,
or the next ...

I will hold onto my love for and memories of
you, forever.

Uncomfortability
4/30/20, nw

Sometimes, I'm uncomfortable with you.
Other times, with myself.
More often, with politics, religion, bigotry,
and the confusing fabrications of human nature.

Frequently, I'm uncomfortable with the weather:
hail storms, fog, hurricanes, tornados . . .
Always with vexing elements of the natural world:
pine sap, mud, black flies, termites . . .

Bottom line?
I am uncomfortable with anything I don't understand,
fail to appreciate, or
(dare I say) misinterpret.

Yet, despite these discomforts,
I fully believe that all created things—
living and nonliving—
serve a purpose.
>Rocks and oceans
rain and wind,
fish and sharks,
apes and humans...
emotions, brain waves,
abilities, disabilities.

Therefore,
if you and all creation
could hear me, I would say:

Forgive me
for feeling uncomfortable,
for misunderstanding,
for under-appreciating,
for judging.

You—the trees, fish, gnats, and ants,
storms, floods, and melting icebergs,
neighbors, family, friends, and associates,
and fabrications of human nature
are in my life…You are my life.

I'm a slow learner
but I have a great Mentor;
and gradually—ever so gradually—
I'm starting to get it.

Bear with me.

Is Trump the Problem?

10/16/17, nw

"TO JOIN IS TO SEPARATE." Although I don't know the author, those words have hit home more than once in my life.
Today a friend posted an anti-Trump sentiment on FaceBook
and I found myself shaking my head in agreement. I wanted to
give her two or three thumbs-up emojis to let her know whose
team I'm on, even though she already knows. Yes, Trump
causes me and many others serious concern, and, yes, I would
like to blame him for everything (and anything)—but what
would my thumbs-up emoji or a "You go, girl!" comment to
her FB post accomplish? It would join me with one group and
separate me from another. And how is that a positive thing?

The bottom line is that my negative or positive estima-
tion of Donald Trump symbolizes bigger issues on a personal as well as a global level. On the personal level, I am angry
and frustrated with those who take a different view of Trump,
aligning me with some and separating me from others. On the
global level, Trump's fame or infamy represents an unsettled
world.

We proud Americans coming out of the twentieth centu-
ry cannot remember a time when the United States was not
the most influential power in the world; the good guy; the
wearer of the white hat. Yet since long before the election of
2016, we've been watching our country become more divid-
ed and, consequently, more weakened. And around the globe,
two hundred million people are in need of humanitarian aid,
including over 65 million refugees, yet the global agenda leans
more toward anti-immigration and isolationism. Terrorism is
rampant. Nuclear war is suddenly more of a possibility than it
has been in 60 years. Climate change is more evident, yet more

controversial than ever before in the wind, rain, fire, and life everywhere.

These realities, these fears, fill a brewing pot we call our world. The bubbles on the surface (like Trump, Harvey Weinstein, Bashar al-Assad, Putin. . .) symbolize the fire, the source of heat beneath the surface. (How's that for metaphor?)

And what is the source of the fire beneath the surface? Beneath the telltale bubbles? Human ideology. That which distinguishes Homo sapiens from all other species: our unique ability to reason, imagine, contemplate, create, influence, govern, abuse, persecute, destroy, and, ultimately, obliterate. The past, present, and future events of history are the consequences (good and bad) of human ideology.

Trump may be a symbol—a bubble on the surface—but his election to the presidency of the United States is a consequence of evolving human ideology. Britain's vote to leave the European Union is a consequence of human ideology. Catalonia's desire to succeed from Spain, North Korea's proclivity to nuclear war, [Russia's invasion of Ukrainia], Dachau, slavery, war, persecution, discrimination, feudalism, paganism, religion, the Tower of Babel . . . All are consequences of human ideology—every bit as much as the Nobel Peace Prize, the moon landing, the invention of penicillin, democracy, and computer technology.

So . . . if I post or respond to a pro- or anti-Trump sentiment—real or fake—on social media, am I improving a broken and unsettled world? Or am I contributing to it? Am I advancing a better ideology or jeopardizing one? Am I a better person? Am I less biased? Am I happier?

I can't move forward, I can't have a positive influence, I can't help others if I am shrouded in an anti-anything mentality or ideology. What to do, then, in the age of Trump and the one percent and assault weapons and terrorism and trade wars and climate change?

Here's my attempt at an answer . . . and a personal goal: Focus on what can be made better and what can be fixed within the arena of my own life, first. Stare negativity in the face, then turn and walk in the other direction—but walk with a purpose and with an open-mind. Seek out truth; abstain from negativism; represent the ethical and moral high ground. If I feel the need to speak, or march, or activate for a purpose and for change, do it without condescension, without a dualistic attitude; focus on the purpose, on the greater good . . . not the opposition.

Certainly easier said than done! If only my instincts weren't so finitely human!

"A voice within us calls out, 'This is wrong and cannot stand.'
We yearn for a world in which all can flourish.
Fueled by our own particular yearning, we occasionally
entertain visions for how some small part of our world can be
liberated into greater possibility."

(Rabbi Nahum Ward-Lev)

"If I look at the masses, I will never act.
If I look at the one, I will."

(Mother Teresa)

FAITH

"Doubt is not the opposite of faith; it is one element of faith."
(Paul Tillich)

*"It is not only in the thought of philosophers or the
contemplation of mystics—but in the general consciousness
of humankind—that the awareness of some divine presence
underlying evolution demands to be clearly recognized as
an ultimate and constant support for action."*

(Pierre Teilhard de Chardin, *Science and the Christ*)

Approaching Omega
Thoughts about my journey of faith

3/16/16, nw

APPROACHING MY SEVENTIETH YEAR of life, I find the concept of my inevitable end—as well as the possible end of all human life on earth—to be logical, intriguing, and reassuring. A hard-fought understanding that has been a long time coming.

From my youth growing up in the Protestant tradition, I believed in a God-ordained beginning to the universe as comfortably as I believed that I was somehow created by God. My family went to church regularly and, though we rarely talked about God in our home, God's existence and somehow God's involvement in our world were taken for granted. Death, however, was too abstract and the idea of a God-ordained end to earth and human life was an uncomfortable and suspicious theory.

As a college student in the late 1960s, I put any thoughts of God on a distant back-burner; a belief or trust in God seemed too simplistic and naïve in a world at war in Viet Nam and at odds with my baby-boomer-upbringing.

In my early twenties, I was struggling through a post-college identity crisis when my dad died suddenly of a heart attack; events that just happened to coincide with the Jesus movement of the early 1970s. I was intrigued with conversations about life after death and the "endtimes," and found myself praying "the sinner's prayer" before I knew what hit me.

For the next 35 years, I was immersed in conservative evangelical Christianity, pretty much believing everything I was told by people I considered to be "more mature Christians" than me. In the early years of my "born-again" status,

I couldn't get enough of God, even going to the extreme of attending an evangelical seminary where I earned a Master's Degree in Theological Studies.

I married a fellow seminarian/evangelical Christian. Our marriage was to be a "biblically-based" union, with my husband serving as the head-of-the-household and my attempt at being a subservient wife—not something at which I excelled. The marriage began to flounder sometime after the first decade—despite the prayers and advice of many "fellow believers"—but we stuck it out for 24 years.

The gradual dissolution of our marriage and its dissonance with evangelical Christianity forced me to start thinking for myself about the essence of truth and the profundities of life. I awoke to the realization that instead of trusting God, I had been trusting the doctrines, teachings, and biblical interpretations of a group of people for the last three decades of my life. My awareness of this irony led to what my then husband and my church community saw with concern as a failure on my part to obey and submit to biblical authority.

Try as they would to pull me "back into the fold", I desperately needed to escape. I was overwhelmed with doubts about a faith which gradually stagnated over my years of submission to the teachings and doctrines of conservative Christianity. The church I was leaving considered my doubts almost heretical—a frowned-upon form of disbelief.

Now, outside "the walls" with the freedom to doubt, I found myself allowing questions long sequestered to be voiced to a God I no longer feared, and soon I discovered writings and voices that opened my mind. My doubts were profoundly influenced by a writer, scientist, and Jesuit priest named Pierre Teilhard de Chardin in his classic early twentieth-century writing, "Le Phenomene Humain" (originally given the

English title of "The Phenomenon of Man," now referred to as "The Human Phenomenon")[1]. As the title indicates, his book focuses on the totally unique and unparalleled emergence of Homo sapiens in the earth's evolutionary process. (In my previous, evangelical life, the subject of evolution was taboo. Teilhard and other newly discovered writers allowed me to breathe again.)

Teilhard made a concerted effort to justify his deep spiritual beliefs with his scientific research and discipline as a paleontologist (even to the point of allowing the Roman Catholic Church to suppress the publication of his work until after his death). In his writings he associates a divine creation of earth with a scientific beginning; a cosmic "accident", occurring hundreds of millions of years ago, followed by the development of layers, such as the barysphere (metallic layer), lithosphere (rock layer), hydrosphere (liquid), atmosphere (air), and biosphere (life).

But it is with the "noosphere" and "hominization", terms Teilhard coined in 1925, that the phenomenon of human life begins. These terms refer to the emergence of intelligence, thought, reflection, and belief in things not seen—attributes unique to the human species.

Teilhard refers to evolution as "an ascent towards consciousness." In the arc between a divinely-ordained beginning (which Teilhard refers to as the "Alpha Point") and a divinely-ordained eventual end (his "Omega Point"), the emergence of human reflection and knowledge (hominization) is at the apex, drawing life thereafter toward ultimate meaning, understanding, and fulfillment of purpose.

Teilhard, the Jesuit priest and paleontologist, cautions "the upholders of the spiritual explanation" (e.g., biblical creationists, I assume) to not be worried when they are "obliged to see" the great apes compared to humans. He refers to the story of life as a movement of consciousness veiled by morphology, implying that evolution must lead to "some sort of supreme consciousness."

As he approaches his conclusions, Teilhard refers to the human draw to research and to the unification of science and religion. He says that humans "will only continue to work and to research so long as [they are] prompted by a conviction, strictly undemonstrable to science, that the universe has a direction…"

And this is the author's premise and key: *That the universe has a direction* . . . a belief in progress toward "some sort of irreversible perfection".

Teilhard implies that the progression of certain properties in the human race (i.e., invention, attraction/repulsion, and incorruptibility) reveal that we are moving toward "a critical pole of reflection of a collective and higher order"—toward "that transcendent focus we call Omega."

I believe—and Teilhard implies—that not only is God drawing all of humanity forward to a greater consciousness, but that God is drawing each of us individually forward in a personal journey, from an early alpha to a perhaps late-blooming omega point; to gradual and greater understanding of a truth which our finite minds are not meant to fully comprehend on this side of eternity.

In faith lies the mysterious, the supernatural, the existence of things unseen . . . concepts that some people consciously or sub-consciously avoid at all costs. And here is where my life-long struggle with low self-esteem becomes a blessing in disguise. If I deny that the universe has a direction, a pull toward some sort of mysterious "irreversible perfection," then I deny that human life in general and my own individual life in particular have purpose, meaning, or significance.

Only in the concluding chapters of his book does Teilhard directly touch on Christian theology. Our universe, he says, labors, sins, and suffers. He concludes his appendix and his book with these words: "In one manner or the other it still remains true that, even in the view of the mere biologist, the human epic resembles nothing so much as a way of the Cross."

The "way of the cross" is the Christian analogy of Jesus walking through the streets of Jerusalem to his place of execution on a hill outside the city, carrying the wooden cross on which he was to be executed. The cross represents the sin and suffering of the world, of humanity. Jesus' death on the cross represented God's total identification with our pain and suffering.

I can no longer accept the common Christian statement I once embraced: that "Christ died to save us from our sins." God has loved us from the beginning of humanity despite our sins. Jesus wasn't "Plan B"—God's solution for a humanity that went bad. Jesus (I believe) was the always planned human incarnation in Plan A, which began 13.8 billion years ago with the *first* incarnation of God in the creation of the universe. At this point in my life I would interpret "the way of the cross" to mean that we, like Jesus, must carry the sins of humanity with us to the end—to the end of my life and to the end of human life—even if it is our sins which bring about the end.

Is sin "failure"? Yes, and failure is the antithesis of perfection and God is perfection. But Teilhard is implying that somewhere in route to our demise, we will approach an eternal comprehension, a faith, strength, purpose, and readiness for what Omega means: knowing God.

If Alpha includes preparation for a beginning (i.e., the Big

Bang, gestation, birth), then Omega means preparation for an ending (i.e., aging, contemplating death, dying, the end of human life, eternal life).

I personally believe that humanity, in the aggregate, will journey towards an Omega Point. But on the individual level, one might wonder how Teilhard's Omega theory relates to those who, during their lifetime, insist there is no God.

And what does God do with the minds and souls of those people we finite humans go so far as to call "evil"—seemingly beyond redemption? Hitler, Stalin, Putin, etc?

Fortunately, questions that remain beyond our finite comprehension are still in the realm of an incomprehensible Love.

*Words in quotes represent a language I used to speak with biased pride, but now carefully avoid.

Choices and Choosings

2/3/07, nw

(Revised and emboldened significantly—just like me—many times over the years, until 4/14/22)

I have beliefs, I have doubts,
I have faith, I have questions,
and I have choices.

I believe (without doubt)
that every human, every creature,
every tree, every raindrop, every atom and molecule
on every continent, in every sea on earth and beyond
has been created and purposed by a loving God.
And I am one of those loved creations.

Once, long ago, I was told
that I was among those "chosen" by God.
"Chosen" for "salvation," heaven, eternal life—
was my understanding.
Synonyms like "predestined," "called," "elect"
were there in Scripture (like it or not).

And so, for many years I basked in this understanding,
feeling honored, special, "chosen,"
as I "fellowshipped" with other "believers."
I shared this understanding ("the Gospel")
with "non-believers"
in hopes of pulling them (the opposite of us)
into the fold.

Over time, however, doubts emerged.
I found myself questioning what I had long been told,
and I realized my discomfort with dualistic thinking:
us and them; "believers" and "non-believers";
"chosen" and . . . unchosen . . . ?

If I am among God's "chosen"
are there others left rejected?
(Unqualified for "salvation"??)

If every creature and creation
is loved by the Creator,
why would the Creator choose some and not all? And
how does the Grace of God enter into God's "choosing"?

Did God's choosing cause my faith?
Or did my faith cause God to choose me?

Weren't we, as humans, endowed by God with free will?
Free choice? If one has the choice to look at God,
why not the choice, as well, to look away?
By questioning a doctrine of faith,
am I looking away from God?

And if one looks away—their back to God
(likened to the sun behind one's body)—
do shadows fall?
Does darkness loom?
Can the grace of God exist in places darkened by one's choice?

Can one choose to be set free from "sin" and darkened places,
or is release by virtue of God's choosing?

Does one return to God by conscious choice—
or chosen status?
Can I lose my chosen status?
Can God reject those chosen?

Again I ask:
Would the God of all creation
choose some but not all of creation?
No. A loving parent chooses all of their children.
Even those who rebel.

Are those who proclaim different faiths
or no particular faith
not "chosen"?
Would a loving parent deny
those of differing political beliefs
or life choices?

Evolving faith.
Unceasing doubts.
Continuous questions
And choices . . .

All part of a journey,
a perpetual quest,
with deepening awareness that
my questions are indeed heard
and encouraged—

not by a religion, a doctrine, a church,
a pastor, a priest or a rabbi—
but by a mysterious, regenerating source of Love in my life

whom I refer to as God
but who answers to many names.

In this, my journey of faith,
I am lured and assured,
pulled and pushed,
seared and refined …
and continually transformed.

This I choose.

---

*Words in quotes represent a language I used to speak with biased pride, but now carefully avoid.

The Blessings of Uncertainty

5/13/15, nw

Uncertainty means that what I have long believed to be true might not be true after all. How does my acceptance of (and gratitude for) the reality of uncertainty impact my life, my actions, and my ever-evolving faith? What has come into my realm of thinking that is influencing my broadening perspective?

Here's a good example: One of the most oft-cited of Jesus' parables is the Parable of the Lost Sheep (Matthew 18:12-14; Luke 15:3-7), in which a shepherd—faithfully guarding his flock—realizes that one sheep has wandered away. I (and perhaps most people) have always assumed that the good shepherd of this story was God (or God-incarnate, i.e., Jesus) and the lost sheep was me (or any other confused human).

It has been suggested, however, that I consider what this parable would mean if the lost sheep represented Jesus or God, instead of me—which would make me (yikes!) the shepherd; the one expected to take responsibility.

But . . . I don't *want* to be the one expected to take responsibility (in this or any other parable, for that matter)! I would much prefer to be the sheep and be assured that Jesus or God as the good shepherd will be coming after me should I stray from the metaphorical flock.

If Jesus in this allegory/parable represents a lost soul, my responsibility as the shepherd would be to go out of my way—beyond the normal call of a shepherd's duty, leaving the 99 reliable, manageable, compliant sheep—to try to communicate with one whom I might see as confused... screwed up... not too bright... self-centered... unable to see the light or make a wise decision... succumbing to temptation... or just plain defiant.

It would be SO much easier and more practical and definitely preferable, for me/the shepherd to stick with the 99 who get it—heaping praise on them for their societal compliance—than to have to deal with one recalcitrant. However, if Jesus/God, represents the lost sheep, I am certainly not going to think of him as "recalcitrant" or one who is defiant or "screwed up".

This is getting complicated. Why would Jesus put himself (metaphorically-speaking) in the place of a lost sheep??

The late theologian Robert Farrar Capon posed this challenge in his book "Kingdom, Grace, Judgment: Paradox, Outrage, and Vindication in the Parables of Jesus"[2], focusing on Matthew 25:40: "Whatever you did for one of the least of these brothers and sisters of mine, you did for me."

In another example—the Parable of The Good Samaritan (Luke 10:25-37)—Capon turns the tables again and encourages us to see Jesus not as the Good Samaritan I have always thought he was supposed to represent, but as the poor sucker traveling from Jerusalem to Jericho who was attacked by robbers, beaten, stripped of his clothes, and left for dead.

Jesus, according to Capon, represents himself in his parables as the unfortunate, the lost, the loser, the beaten, the weak. He is not the heroic messiah we (and the Jews of his day) want him to be. His strategy, says Capon, is not "right-handed", knock-'em down, in-your-face-victory as we typically think of victories, but "left-handed," turn the other cheek, meekness and seeming weakness.

So, if I am to see the beggars and losers and lost souls and victims in my journey through life as if I were looking at Jesus-the-incarnate-God ... how would I treat them? Would I ignore them as the priest and the Levite did when they passed the naked, beaten man in the parable of the Good Samaritan—or would I stop and care for them?

Well, of course I would like to think that I would stop and help someone who had been left for dead (although standards, ethics, and expectations were different 2,000 years ago on the road to Jericho; now we could just call 911 and be on our way without having to get involved). Would I go out of my way to help him, as the Good Samaritan did, applying salve to his wounds, putting him in my nice clean Subaru, taking him to the nearest emergency room, and expending my hard-earned money to help him? Would I willingly miss my important appointment and all my other self-focused plans for the day to care for someone I didn't even know? This could screw up everything! It could affect my plans and activities for tomorrow; it could cause tension within my family or friendships or work environment. It could change my life!

Clearly there seems to be a lot of emphasis on ME in these possible scenarios. What about the person who was beaten and left for dead who happens to be in my path? (If only I had taken Route 95 instead of Route 3 to Jericho, this never would have been an issue! But I didn't, did I?)

What about Jesus? No, not, "What would Jesus do?", but what should I do for this poor molested person in my path, whom I should be seeing as the Messiah, the hope for the world?

And then it begins to dawn on me that there are a lot of hurting, unfortunate, misunderstood people in my path each day that I would prefer to avoid (or, at least, not notice) so I could get on with my plans. Is it all about my plans, or might there be a greater, more purposeful plan?

I remember back to when I worked for the NH Department of Corrections, being bothered by an inmate's wife (Ms.

Nunez), who called every day to ask if we had received her husband's application for Administrative Home Confinement, a status that would allow him to leave prison on an ankle bracelet. It got to be so annoying, that when I would hear her voice (she had a difficult to understand Hispanic accent), I would think to myself: "Oh, no, not you again! Stop bothering me! I've got more important work to do!"

Of course, I didn't say those things to her, but my attitude was probably evident in my responding tone of voice. But what if this poor, English-impaired, wife of a convicted felon was . . . Jesus/God-incarnate (in disguise)?

The point being that I should think of her as Jesus or God-incarnate. Or even her husband—a convicted felon who broke the law and maybe even hurt other people—as Jesus. Yet Jesus wouldn't (couldn't) break the law because he is God incarnate . . . so why am I putting myself through this line of reasoning??!! Why don't I just conveniently forget to see Jesus/God in others? Especially in the unfortunates who get in my path!

Because . . . now that I've realized that God wants me to stop and see God/Jesus in others, I can't not do it. Well . . . that is, I could try . . . I could try real hard not to think of Jesus in the poor unfortunate person in my path. But, you know how it is going back to the old way of doing things once you've been enlightened?

I remember delighting in 4th of July fireworks reflecting over my favorite lake until the day I learned that firework residue in the lake poisons the (cute little) fish and other living organisms there. Why did someone have to point out the negative? The unfortunate? The weak?

Why couldn't I just think of that convicted felon or the misguided woman who married him as . . . as . . . non-believers, non-humanity? If they were good people, people of deep/ sincere faith, they would have known better, right?

Wrong. I have made myriad mistakes and wrong choices in my life . . . wrong choices that have changed my world and my life, as well as the lives of others. I have done things and said things (although I'm not exactly sure which things) that have caused my daughter to sever her relationship with me. It doesn't get much uglier than that.

I have been the "lost sheep," the recalcitrant who is confused, screwed up, not too bright, self-centered, depressed, unable to see the light or make a wise decision, succumbing to temptation, or just plain defiant. And I am as susceptible to confusion as the homeless beggar on the street or the addict in rehab or the lost sheep. I am flawed and fallible. And, now that my mind has been opened to the "blessing" of uncertainty, I feel compelled to act on these revelations.

In my ever-evolving journey of faith, replete with myriad questions and doubts, I have come to understand that God became human for a brief period of history 2,000 years ago NOT to be the victorious white knight or the Good Shepard, and not to create a religion called Christianity with all of its cathedrals, power, corruption, and conflicting doctrines—but to identify with, suffer with, and show love and compassion for the "lost sheep" . . . for us . . . for humanity and all of creation.

Jesus came so that our eyes might be opened to the true meaning of God's love, so that we—all humanity—might be instruments of that love in the lives of others and on the earth we have inherited.

What Then?

4/26/97, nw

Inevitable death.
What then?
What if the soul lives on
and meets its maker?

Once there, on the other side of life,
might a soul explain to God:
"I was good.
I went to church.
My oversights were few.
God of Love,
accept me into your kingdom."

And God responds:
"Now you will know Me,
you will understand all things.
Not because you were 'good'
or 'went to church,'
but because I have always loved you."

An atheist arrives, with trepidation.
"You were there all along!
"Why was I so blind?"

And God responds:
"Now you will know Me;
You will understand all things.
Despite your long denial,
I have always loved you."

Another soul arrives
confessing sin.
"My life on earth was hard.
I sold my body; I stole for drugs.
As I breathed my last, I heard you say:
'Today you will be with me in Paradise.'"

And God responds:
"Now you will know Me;
you will understand all things,
because you died a sinner's death
and saw Me.
And because I have always loved you."

"But," one asks,
"are there those beyond redemption?
Perhaps without a soul?
A Hitler, a Stalin, [a Putin]?
Are there some irrevocably warped?
Is anyone
outside of the love of God?"

How can we sing while in a foreign land?

1/15/07, nw

"How can we sing while in a foreign land?"
the psalmist asked.
How can my eyes see God
When my back is turned?

Who am I calling out to
when my heart is cold?
Not to you, Lord,
but to an audience imagined.

(cf, Psalm 137:4)

Love Enduring
2/20/14, nw

One day there entered a glimmer of love
through a portal I had all but obstructed.

His subject line described our meeting as "Delightful."
He cared!

Like me, he needed to give love and be loved.
And so he loved a person with crumbled self-esteem
back to a place of hope.

He had lost a wife of 40 years.
What does he need?
What can I give?

Enter love.
Two spirits rising.

*"If only our eyes saw souls instead of bodies,
how different our ideals of beauty would be."*

(Lauren Jauregui)

*"Judge tenderly, if you must. There is usually a side you have
not heard, a story you know nothing about,
and a battle waged that you are not having to fight."*

(Traci Lea Larussa)

KINDNESS

"A man is but the product of his thoughts.
What he thinks, he becomes."

(Mahatma Gandhi)

"Some things are better left unsaid, which I generally realize
right after I have said them."

(nw)

Kindness or The Absence Thereof
4/18/17, nw

I ADMIT THAT I'M OVERLY SENSITIVE. Some who know me would say that's an understatement. My over-sensitivity may explain why self-esteem has always been a challenge for me to locate (or maybe my low self-esteem is the cause of my over-sensitivity?). So . . . read on only if you've ever felt Unliked or Unfairly Judged.

A sunny day—literally and figuratively—makes me happy and content and at peace with the world without having to think about why. It's like an unsolicited hug. But when darkness encroaches, I forget how the sunshine feels. Warmth recedes. For me, the sense of darkness is almost always related to an absence or withdrawal of kindness or even a downright act of unkindness or rudeness—usually by another person but, often enough, by me. When it's done to me, I feel unliked, unfairly judged . . . and rather worthless. When I realize I have done it to someone else, I'm ashamed.

Either way, my self-esteem plunges and the sun stops shining for a while.

Why are we sometimes unkind to other people and why are other people sometimes unkind to us?

Here are some possibilities: We might dislike what a person or group of people represent (e.g., politically, religiously, philosophically, ethnically, racially, sexually, etc.)—usually referred to as judgmentalism. Or we may dislike what someone is doing or saying at the moment (e.g., using profanity, speaking condescendingly or arrogantly, etc.). Possibly we are reciprocating a perceived act of unkindness or judgmentalism.

Is unkindness always intentional? Can innocent actions

on my part be misconstrued as unkindness by another? If I am on the receiving end of what feels like unkindness, does that always mean an unkindness has been intentionally perpetrated? If it feels like someone has "slapped" me, should I slap back? Or should I turn the other cheek, allowing for another slap, and then slink away into a dark place?

I have been the recipient as well as the proponent of unkindness. With this journaled analysis, I am considering both issues as they pertain to me. I can't change other people, but I can try to change myself—and, hopefully, find more self-esteem in the process. A sociologist or psychologist or behavioral specialist would approach this more scientifically and objectively. My only credentials are my finite curiosity and a desire to seek my God-given potential.

Regarding my own acknowledged guilt of unkindness to others, I find that it is almost always triggered by my reaction to something or someone. The minute I hear my tone of voice go south or feel my nostrils flare or realize a desire to do unto someone as they have done unto me, I am susceptible.

I'm talking to my cousin on the phone and he starts mocking a mentally challenged person . . .

A person who frequently says things that I perceive to be rude or thoughtless or childish enters my path . . .

In each case my defenses are up. My teeth are clenched. My attitude has changed. And nothing's even transpired yet.

Leslie glares at me; I glare back. Arnold's tone of voice is harsh; I respond in kind. Megan rolls her eyes; I arch my back and cock my head.

Sometimes, when confronted with our own acts of unkindness or rudeness, we write it off. We think: "It's really not intentional. We live busy lives. People can be inept; obtuse;

ignorant; foolish. We react; we move on. What's the big deal?"

With this line of thinking I'm saying, "I wouldn't be un-kind to you, my friend, but that lady who's unloading a full grocery cart in the 14-Items-or-Less lane? I am giving her "The Look." In fact, the checkout clerk is also getting "The Look," because he shouldn't be letting that happen! I am in a hurry! Maybe I'll just go over there and tell them what I think!"

Unintentional?

Unkindness—whether retribution, frustration, or mere absence of respect—is usually (I'll stop short of saying always) intentional, and carries with it the possibility of making a person (especially the overly sensitive type) feel unliked, unfairly judged, or unappreciated. In fact, it could cast a veil over the rest of their day.

In contrast, we might want to think that kindness or respect should (at least in a perfect world) be instinctual, habitual. Wouldn't that be nice? But, unfortunately, we don't live in a perfect world; kindness needs to be practiced . . . daily.

"That's a nice color on you, Joan."

"I'm sorry I haven't always been there for you, Alex. How can I make it up?"

"I know you've been through quite an ordeal, Peter. Are you doing OK?"

Practiced kindness. Some people practice more effort-lessly than others.

Often the absence of kindness or an act of unkindness can be the result of preconceived judgmentalism, which usually infers negative opinions of others. Acting on or speaking such negative judgments usually produces unkindness.

If I like a person or a group of people, I judge them kindly. As an advocate for the homeless I might think: "That poor homeless man doesn't stand a chance of being heard." If I were to follow that judgment with an action, it would be one of kindness, such as going over and talking to him.

If I don't like a person (or a group of people), my judgment might be: "What a liar!" or "What a self-righteous religion!" And, if I allow such thoughts or opinions to impact my behavior, my proclivity would <u>not</u> be toward kindness. White supremacists, for example, are rarely kind to people of color.

What to do? Probably best to avoid such interactions whenever possible—but, make a mental note to give serious thought to why I (not why others, but why I) am judgmental in the first place? Why, for example, don't I like white supremists? First of all, I'm generalizing. I need to think of them as individuals, not a group of bad people. Like me, they're human beings; they were babies and toddlers and teenagers . . . and, like me, they formed judgments . . . (So much to think about!)

Now to consider my reaction to being the recipient of perceived unkindness. I can work on being kinder to others, but I cannot prevent someone from being unkind or thoughtless toward me. I can try to change the subject to something more mutually agreeable, but the shadow is cast. I need to address the darkness that descends on me without reciprocating unkindness.

I can go where the sun is shining. Ideally, I would gently excuse myself and move to a different venue: across the room to visit with Bob and Ted and Alice or up the stairs to the bathroom or out the door for a breath of fresh air. If I can't take my physical leave at the moment, I can go to a comforting place in my thoughts.

My over sensitivity and low self-esteem can bring me pretty low when I stand in the absence of kindness. But, fortunately, before I hit rock bottom, the angel on one shoulder usually whispers louder than the devil on my other shoulder, reminding me that I have *value* whether I see it or not; and that the other guy has value too, even if it's not obvious.

This buoy of believed-though-not-always-seen value is reason enough for me to make a concerted effort to <u>not</u> be unkind, to not be rude, to not stand in judgment—whether or not someone else is unkind or rude or standing in judgment of me. I'm human, therefore I'll fail sometimes, but I'm sensitive, therefore I'm going to keep on trying.

Although I've long felt this way, I am only now finding the need to articulate it. Admitting to something and carefully analyzing it triggers motivational forces in my still evolving personhood. By identifying an issue in my life (e.g., "It is important to me to focus on kindness—even in the absence of kindness by another"), I am making a commitment; establishing an area of accountability; taking off blinders. I am lifting the veil so the sun can shine—at least in my life, and, hopefully, in someone else's as well.

Words and Silence
8/1/16, nw

Words can...
Create value . . . or lower self esteem
Give strength . . . or destroy confidence
Express feelings . . . or dampen spirits
Extend hope . . . or break hearts
Encourage . . . or humiliate
Heal . . . or anger
Help . . . or hurt

Note to self: Before sharing words with another person,
become the receiver.

Silence, on the other hand, can...
Bring peace . . . or elicit angst
Inspire thought . . . or produce melancholy
Offset anger . . . or trigger frustration
Lead to reflection . . . or create confusion
Deflect arrows . . . or inflict pain
Soothe . . . or offend
Help . . . or hurt

Note to self: Before allowing silence, understand the message.

.

Do Good Anyway

5/14/14, nw

Wouldn't it be nice if life were like a boomerang?
The more good you throw out,
the more good you receive in return?

The more kindness you show,
the more love you give;
the more you respect others,
the more appreciation you extend;
the more you accept responsibility,
the more honest you are with other people.
The more your actions *should* be reciprocated.

And, the more you are defined by characteristics such as these,
the better the world around you *should* become.

But sometimes
kindness, love, and respect
are met with anger, jealousy, or awkward silence.

Too often the acceptance of responsibility
results in chastisement or rudeness or separation.

When you are sensitive or honest,
sometimes people become angry or vengeful.

And while we may be defined by positive characteristics,
The world around us remains hostile.

So remember the words of Mother Teresa:

"The good you do today,
some will forget tomorrow;
Do good anyway."

"Give the world the best you have.
Though it may never be enough,
Give the best you've got anyway."

Value or Vacuum
5/22/12, nw

Compassion, presence,
kindness, touch,
a friendly word, a smile, support.

Thoughtfulness produces warmth;
continual warmth radiates love.
Love illuminates value.

When time goes by
without love or warmth,
some of us might sense a vacuum;
a place where value and self-esteem
are hard to find;
perhaps, a wellspring for discouraging thoughts.

If so, then it would seem
that kindness and love
are as important to give
as to receive.

FUN

"The liberal in me can smile at certain things that my mother's very proper daughter would tell me not to."

(nw)

Ah, Scotland!

8/21/19, nw

Where dollars are pounds
And little is wee
Where tiny is tad
And you is ye.

Where yes is aye
And no is nae
A baby's a bairn
A hill is a brae.

Where lakes are lochs
And boys are laddies
TVs are boxes
Potatoes are tatties.

Where pretty is bonnie
Silly is daft
A fool is a dobber
A young girl's a lass.

Where haggis is relished
And shortbread revered
Whiskey's abundant
And scones are endeared.

Where islands are isles
Inlets are firths
Scots are Brits
But not the reverse.

Where proud Highland clans
Flaunt their tartans with flair
Where bagpipes abound
And in Gaelic they swear.

The land of Macbeth
And of Sir Walter Scott
Where Stewarts were kings
But Prince Charlie, not.

Where Mary was Queen
And John Knox was mean
Where Jacobites hailed
But—in the end—failed.

*We enjoyed our week in Scotland with Mark's granddaughter
Laura in June 2019.*

Lazy Mind Syndrome
11/27/13, nw

THE ENGLISH MAJOR IN ME cringes at conversational negligence just as readily as I do when seeing grammatical and punctuation errors in writing. Conversational negligence is evidence of a lazy mind—and I am equally guilty. I am not talking about lack of intelligence; I'm talking about lack of effort in the process of talking.

For example, how often do we hear the following catch-all phrases caught up in conversation:

"When I earn my Ph.D., I'll be qualified for better positions . . . *and stuff like that*."

"I think people want to be recognized for their strength and courage . . . *or whatever*."

"The President's Press Secretary explained that the President wants transparency in his administration . . . *blah, blah, blah* . . . but nothing's changed"

"That's not exactly a flattering color on you . . . *Just sayin'*."

"You **literally** screwed-up."

When I hear other people using phrases like that I become aware that my teeth are clenched. I think to myself: "Why did you even begin to put your thoughts into spoken words if you have to include a catch-all cop-out?" It's a little like finishing a spoken sentence with the words "et cetera, et cetera" (although "et cetera, et cetera" is somehow more tolerable than "and stuff like that" or "blah, blah, blah").

When I hear myself impulsively add on one of those unnecessary idioms, my train of thought is interrupted by my embarrassment at being guilty of my now labeled "lazy mind syndrome."

Phrases such as these are close to but not quite in the same category as what I call conversational extenders, such as "um" and "ya know" and even the cringe-worthy "like." These, in my mind, are just sounds that come out while we're trying to think. . . . which makes them bearable. We all know they wouldn't be included in one's written story (don't we?).

This is exactly why I much prefer to write my thoughts instead of trying to explain them to someone in person. What if my thoughts came out like this:

I don't see any purpose in . . . um . . . continuing a conversation with . . . ya know . . . people who literally can't . . . like . . . complete their thoughts, and stuff like that. But, on the other hand, I am not, like, ready to . . . ya know . . . like, stop talking so that those other people might try to explain their opinions, or . . . um . . . even, like, disagree with me, or . . . whatever. Just sayin' . . .

Rumblings on Earth
A Satire
10/12/18, nw

RUMBLINGS ON EARTH are becoming louder and uglier these days, as if prophetically signaling an explosion or implosion soon to come. Not only does political divide and corruption appear to be invading every corner of our world, but women throughout the earth (yes, not just America, if one can believe that) are daring—with unprecedented boldness—to speak up and act out in non-submissive ways.

For obvious reasons this is causing great alarm, especially in orthodox religious communities. "God, as we know," said an evangelical Christian spokesman recently, "created Man in His image, giving him a penis with which to sow his oats and a tongue with which to tell alternative facts. And, ever since, men have been men (as it should be) in order to be moved into high positions of power.

"Women, on the other hand," this unnamed spokesman went on to say, "were created from the rib of Adam and they should not forget that!"

Why then—we must wonder—are women surprised when they are ridiculed and shamed and disbelieved for telling accusatory stories about sexual harassment and assault and bias in their lives? And why are other women chiming in with "Me too?" You'd think they would be embarrassed to admit it!

Men can justifiably say "I don't remember" to the things that women cannot forget, because our patriarchal God has blessed men with memory loss in order that they might rise to power without feelings of conscience, and exhibit unconflicted headship over women.

"Adam's ribbers," as this Christian gentleman lightheartedly refers to women, "should learn their place in the world that our Father God created . . . along with people of color, refugees of war and famine and political unrest, people who can't seem to identify with heterosexuality, the poverty-stricken and mentally-handicapped, and other non-privileged people that our God, for some reason, also created.

"I believe that our God created the human race to be 50 percent male 'headship' quality and 50 percent submissive female," this spokesman went on to say, adding, "But, it has come to be that—regardless of gender—only One Percent of all people (in these current times) appear to have real worth—and, therefore, real rights. And, as we know, only those who have worth does Our God call 'His Own'."

This spokesman joins others who appear to be quoting from a portion of some scripture recently contributed to and not yet canonized, yet growing in acceptance among privileged Caucasian American Evangelicals (and perhaps certain other orthodox religious sects), paticularly of the male gender.

Things I Can Live Without

8/4/15, nw

Things that I can live without:
Insects, snakes, and sauerkraut.
Pollen, rodents, weeds, and worms;
Vermin, parasites, and germs.

Schemers, screamers, scoffers, smirkers;
Swindlers, shysters, stalkers, shirkers.
Slackers, hackers, spammers, scammers,
Telemarketers and shammers.

Advocates for the NRA,
Donald Trump and the KKK.
The Kardashians and Miley Cyrus,
Fox News and the Covid Virus.

Fractured grammar, hackneyed writings,
Mindless chatter, txt spell sightings;
Punctuation dereliction,
Un-researched historical fiction.

Egotism. Atheism. Botulism. Chauvinism.
Detrimental criticism. Narcissism. Masochism.
Judgmentalism. Anarchism. Fatalism. Favoritism.
Communism. Racism. Ultra-conservatism.

Things that I can live without
could fill a book, without a doubt.
But most of all I rue the time
spent forcing words to make them rhyme.

What Fruit Flies Know

10/2/19, nw

Its life began in dirt,
unplanned and undetected,
quietly emerging through a hole
in the back of our compost bin.

Maybe the fruit flies knew
and some curious worms and ants,
but inside our house a few feet away
no one suspected.

One day, while adding peelings
to the compost bin,
my husband noticed a tiny gourd
on a leafy vine
curling from behind.

We showed the grandkids
who thought it very curious.
We watched and touched,
and wrinkled up our noses.

And, as the summer ended,
my husband cut it from its vine
and carried it inside.
There he carved and hallowed out
the unplanned token of our compost,
revealing a fruit every bit as inviting and nourishing
as if planted with intention.

A Final Word

*"My words sound better coming from my hands
than from my mouth."*

(Unknown)

*"The reason to write is to get the information out of your head
and heart and into the head and heart of others."*

(John Casimir O'Keefe)

A Final Word

4/22/24, nw

A Book?
Self-publishing a book about me and my thoughts?
Who the heck do I think I am, anyway?

I am an average person
yet unique, like every snowflake.
One thing that makes me unique
is my need to write.
Sometimes I think too much
and have to put those thoughts on paper
to unclutter my brain
and understand my heart.
And also because I don't know how better to say
"Listen," or "Here's a thought," or "Could this be true?"
or "What is my heart trying to say?"

When I speak, it never comes out quite right—
but if I put black words on white paper,
editing—always editing,
my questioning mind seems to make more sense.

I could continue to keep those written thoughts
hidden in a file on my computer
to be tossed when I die, but
I have decided to
let a representative few
slip out for you to read—
hopefully, to better understand me
. . . and what makes us all unique.

Acknowledgments

With this book, I'm ready to relax and enjoy my Omega stage. I've expressed myself, revealed myself, and admitted to my idiosyncrasies. I will continue to read voraciously, volunteer happily, take long nature walks, contemplate the spiritual, appreciate good friendships, and journal my thoughts. I'm well settled in to being a septuagenarian—which wouldn't be at all comfortable or delightful without my husband Mark. He reminds me that I have meaning and purpose, he loves me, and he even likes my writing.

Many thanks also to my cousin and spiritual mentor Patti, my intellectually stimulating brother-in-law Ken, my good friend and detail-oriented editor Deb, my good friend and deep-thinking neighbor Lindy, my good friend and therapist-substitute Pat, and my heart-with-the-homeless soulmate Doug. Thank you all for reading early versions of this book and making the final version possible.

About the Author

Nancy Wolcott is a graduate of Pennsylvania State University with a Bachelor of Arts in English, and of Gordon Conwell Theological Seminary, with a Master of Arts in Theological Studies. Before retiring, Nancy worked in the field of publication editing and design. She lives in Franklin, New Hampshire, with her husband Mark.

She is also the author of *"Tell Me About God: A Book About the God of All Faiths for Children of All Ages."*

Feel free to email her with feedback or just thoughts on what makes us all unique: nancy.wolcott.47@gmail.com.

Endnotes

1. Pierre Teilhard de Chardin, *The Phenomenon of Man* (New York: Harper Collins, 2008)

2. Robert Farrar Capon, *Kingdom, Grace, Judgment: Paradox, Outrage, and Vindication in the Parables of Jesus* (Grand Rapids, Michigan: William B. Eerdmans, 2002)